GERMANY

Mike Hirst

RSVP
RAINTREE
STECK-VAUGHN
PUBLISHERS
A Steck-Vaughn Company

Austin, Texas
www.steck-vaughn.com

Other titles:

Brazil • The Caribbean • China • France • India • Israel
Italy • Japan • Kenya • Mexico • West Africa

Cover photograph: A German delicatessen counter showing many different types of meat

Title page: Traditional German meats and cheeses

Contents page: Musicians, dressed up for the festival of *Carnival,* in Cologne

Published by Raintree Steck-Vaughn Publishers, an imprint of Steck-Vaughn Company

Printed in Italy. Bound in the United States.
1 2 3 4 5 6 7 8 9 0 04 03 02 01 00

Library of Congress Cataloging-in-Publication Data
Hirst, Mike.
Germany / Mike Hirst.
     p.   cm.—(Food and festivals)
Includes bibliographical references and index.
Summary: Discusses some of the foods enjoyed in Germany and describes special foods that are part of such specific celebrations as Carnival, Oktoberfest, and Christmas. Includes recipes.
ISBN 0-7398-1372-2
1. Germany—Social life and customs—20th century—Juvenile literature.
2. Food habits—Germany——Juvenile literature.
3. Cookery, German—Juvenile literature.
4. Holidays—Germany—Juvenile literature.
[1. Cookery, German. 2. Food habits—Germany.
3. Festivals—Germany. 4. Holidays—Germany. 5. Germany—Social life and customs]
I. Title. II. Series.
DD67.H57   1999
394.1'0943—dc21   99-30883

CONTENTS

Germany and Its Food

DENMARK

NORTH SEA

BALTIC SEA

N

NETHERLANDS

BELGIUM

LUX

FRANCE

SWITZERLAND

POLAND

CZECH REPUBLIC

AUSTRIA

GERMANY

Hamburg

Weser

Elbe

Berlin

Rhine

Cologne

Frankfurt am Main

Nuremberg

BAVARIA

Danube

Munich

Zugspitze

GERMANY

Germany's place in the world

0   100   200 km

0   100 miles

WHEAT AND RYE

Wheat and rye are both grain crops. They are made into flour, which is used to make bread. Most Germans eat bread twice a day or more.

DAIRY PRODUCTS

Milk, butter, cheeses, and yogurt are popular dairy products in Germany. People eat cheese for breakfast and supper.

FISH

Fish are caught in the sea off the north coast of Germany. Some fish also come from rivers and lakes. Bismarck herrings are popular German fish dishes.

GRAPES

Grapes are grown in vineyards often on the sides of valleys to catch the sun. Many of Germany's grapes are made into wines. German wines are famous all over the world.

MEAT

Many German recipes include meat. Sausages are usually made from pork. There are special rules that say exactly how sausages should be made.

VEGETABLES

Germans eat many different kinds of vegetables. Potatoes and cabbage, which grow well in a cool climate, are often found in traditional cooking.

Food and Farming

▼ In the countryside, some families have worked on the same small farm for two to three hundred years.

With more than 80 million people, Germany is one of the biggest countries in Europe. It has busy towns and cities and large areas of beautiful countryside. Between the flat coast in the north and the high mountains of the south, there are rolling hills, farmland, and thick forests.

Traditional food

▲ An *Imbissstube* is a snack bar that sells traditional food such as sausage.

Germany is a modern, wealthy country, but people still enjoy eating traditional dishes handed down from the past. Wherever you go, from a tiny village to the large capital city of Berlin, you will find someone sitting down to a meal of traditional German food. It might be sausages, *pumpernickel* (a heavy brown bread), or pickled cabbage called *sauerkraut* (pronounced "sour-crout").

FIRST-DAY TREAT

On their first day at school, German children have a special treat: a huge cardboard cone, filled with chocolates and other treats.

BROTPREISE

Doppelbrot	1.20
5er Brezen	3.50
10er Brezen	5.50
Zwiebelbrot	3.—
Vintschgauer	3.—
Wachauerweckerl	
Käsestangen	2.50

Bread and cakes

▲ Pretzels are made of salty dough twisted into a ring shape.

When you go into a German bakery, the first thing you notice is the huge choice of different breads. There are more than 1,200 kinds of rolls, each one made in a slightly different way. Besides bread, many bakeries also sell a large selection of cakes.

ORGANIC FARMING

Organic farmers do not use artificial fertilizers or pesticides on their crops. They feed farm animals natural foods without any extra chemicals. People who eat organic food believe it is healthier and tastes better. Organic food is very popular in Germany.

Most Germans eat some brown bread every day. The flour for this bread is made from grains of wheat or rye, and the mixture includes yeast to make the dough puff up in the oven. Germans also like a heavier type of brown bread, which uses a mixture of sugar and water instead of yeast. This dark brown bread is useful because it stays fresh for a long time: up to three to four weeks.

This photograph shows ▶ a typical evening meal of bread, cold meats, cheese, sauerkraut, and pickles. Many Germans eat their main, hot meal at midday.

Regional food

Every region of Germany, and every big city, has its own special recipes. A *Berliner* is a kind of doughnut, named after the capital city. A frankfurter is a sausage, originally from Frankfurt am Main.

In the coastal towns and cities in the north of the country, fish caught by local boats are widely eaten. Common recipes use herrings, sprats, and mackerel.

Black Forest cake is a delicious confection from the Black Forest in the southwest. In the summer, this region has warm, sunny weather, which is good for growing many kinds of fruit.

DOUGHNUT TROUBLE

In 1963, President John F. Kennedy visited Berlin. He wanted to give his support to the city, so he said "*Ich bin ein Berliner*." He thought this meant "I am a Berliner," but unfortunately, in German, it means "I am a doughnut."

▼ Black Forest cake is flavored with cherries and chocolate.

Food from other lands

Today, many German towns have communities of Turkish or Greek people, who have come to live and work there with their families. They have introduced their own food to Germany. Nowadays, Germans are likely to eat Turkish kebabs and Greek pita bread as well as sausages and sauerkraut.

▲ Stores and restaurants selling Turkish and Greek food are found in many parts of Germany. This take-out store is selling Turkish pizza.

WHAT ARE BISMARCK HERRINGS?

Bismarck herrings are a kind of fish pickled in vinegar. They are named after a famous German chancellor, or prime minister, Otto von Bismarck, who lived from 1815 to 1898. Bismarck's doctor told him that eating the small fish was good for his health, so the chancellor's cook invented a way of keeping them fresh by putting them in vinegar.

Religions and Festivals

Most Germans are Christians. There are two main groups of Christians: Catholics and Protestants. Christmas and Easter are the main Christian festivals, which all Christian Germans celebrate. Different festivals are important for Germany's other religious groups.

▼ These villagers from Bavaria are wearing traditional costumes for a religious festival.

Catholic churches have special services and processions for the holiday of Corpus Christi in June. In November, Protestants have a quiet day of prayer and remembrance, called *Buss und Bettag* (pronounced "Booss oond Bay-tag"). *Buss* means "repentance" and *Bettag* means "quiet thinking."

Many of Germany's Turkish people are Muslims. They celebrate the festivals of Islam, such as Id-ul-Fitr.

Easter

On Easter Sunday, German children hunt around their homes and yards for Easter eggs. They look for eggs that the Easter rabbit has brought for them during the night.

▲ Germans like to paint Easter eggs. The eggs in this picture have traditional patterns painted on them.

Day of Unity

In 1949, four years after the end of World War II, Germany was divided into two separate countries, East Germany and West Germany. It was very difficult to travel between the two countries, and families and friends were split up. On October 3, 1990, the two countries were finally brought back together again. Since then, October 3, has been a holiday for everyone in Germany. It is called "The Day of German Unity."

▼ This dish is called "strength bread." It comes from Hamburg, but today people eat this meal all over Germany. There is a recipe for this dish on the opposite page.

Hamburg "Strength Bread"

EQUIPMENT

Knife
Frying pan
Spatula

INGREDIENTS

1 slice rye bread
Butter or margarine
1 slice ham

1 egg
A little oil for frying
Salt

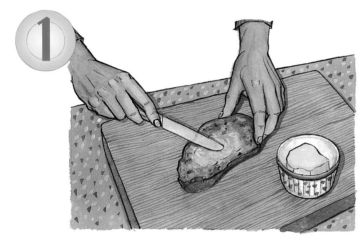

1 Spread a little butter or margarine on the slice of bread.

2 Put the slice of ham on the buttered bread.

3 Ask an adult to heat the oil in the frying pan. Then break the egg into the pan and sprinkle on a pinch of salt.

4 When the egg is cooked, carefully take it out of the pan, and put it on top of the ham.

Always be careful with frying. Ask an adult to help you.

Carnival

Carnival takes place every February, just before the beginning of Lent. For Christians, Lent is a time for quiet thinking and fasting. Some people give up eating a favorite food during Lent, such as desserts.

Before the fasting period of Lent begins, everyone enjoys the parties and parades of *Carnival*.

Marching bands are ▶ an important part of the *Carnival* parades.

16

Carnival begins

The biggest celebration of *Carnival* takes place in the city of Cologne. The festival starts on a Thursday, when the mayor of Cologne hands over the keys of his city to a "Carnival Prince." The next few days are "crazy days," when people have parties and parades. They go out into the streets wearing face paint and costumes. If you walk around the city, you meet clowns, milkmaids, and old-fashioned soldiers.

▼ A band, dressed in rag costumes, plays in front of Cologne cathedral.

Rose Monday Parade

The biggest *Carnival* parade is held on "Rose Monday." More than 7,000 people march through the city with horses, floats, and musicians. People in the parade throw more than 40 tons of candies and 100,000 chocolates into the crowds. The paraders even throw flowers and little containers of Eau-de-Cologne, a kind of perfume made in the city.

The words of a popular *Carnival* folk song say "By Ash Wednesday, it's all over." After such a huge party, everyone is ready for the start of Lent.

▲ Potato pancakes are a specialty from Cologne. They are popular all year round, not just at *Carnival.* There is a recipe for this dish on page 19.

FISH DISHES

One Christian tradition is to stop eating meat during the 40 days of Lent. In Cologne, on Ash Wednesday (the first day of Lent) many restaurants have special fish menus.

Potato Pancakes

INGREDIENTS

2 lb (1 kg) potatoes (new potatoes are best)
1 onion
2 eggs
Pinch of salt
1 cup flour
Pinch of nutmeg
Cooking oil

EQUIPMENT

Potato peeler
Grater
Strainer
Chopping knife

Mixing bowl
Mixing spoon
Frying pan

Peel the potatoes and grate into a strainer, using a rough grater. Leave the potato in the strainer to drain.

Chop the onion fine. Beat the eggs in the bowl. Mix in the onion, grated potatoes, flour, salt, and nutmeg.

Ask an adult to heat the oil gently in a frying pan. Put spoonfuls of the mixture into the pan, and flatten into mini-pancake shapes.

Fry both sides of the cakes until golden brown. Serve hot. Potato pancakes taste good with apple sauce.

Always be careful with chopping and frying. Ask an adult to help you.

Autumn Festivals

Autumn is a time for many local festivals. In the countryside, the harvest is over and people celebrate the end of the hard work. Village churches hold special services of thanksgiving.

▼ The *Oktoberfest* in Munich opens with a colorful procession.

Oktoberfest

The biggest and best-known autumn festival is the *Oktoberfest*, or October Festival. This takes place in the city of Munich and was first held in 1810 to celebrate the wedding of the future king of Bavaria. Today, Bavaria is Germany's largest region, and people in Munich are very proud of their Bavarian traditions.

At *Oktoberfest*, a huge fair is set up, with hundreds of rides and stands. From the top of the massive Ferris wheel, on a clear day, you can see as far as the *Zugspitze* (pronounced "Zoog-shpitsuh"), Germany's highest mountain, far away to the south.

▲ Crowds of people fill the autumn fairground at Munich's *Oktoberfest.*

Festival food

▲ Inside a food tent at the Oktoberfest

Food at the Oktoberfest is served in big tents, where people sit at long wooden tables. They eat pretzels, and sausages are on the menu, too. In Munich, the favorites are white sausage, which you eat by sucking the meat out of the sausage skin. Adults might also have a large glass of beer, made in one of Munich's local breweries. As they eat, visitors listen to folk music, played by a band of wind instruments.

FOOD LAWS

Traditional foods are carefully controlled in Germany. Every type of sausage is made to strict rules, and all beer is made following a special law that was set down in 1516, called the "Purity Law."

◀ White sausage is always served with mustard.

St. Martin's Day

St. Martin's Day, or Martinmas, on November 11, is another autumn festival. It celebrates the legend of St. Martin.

The legend tells how Martin was born into a wealthy family and grew up to be a soldier. One day, he met a beggar who was starving and dying of cold. Martin felt so sorry for the beggar that he took off his own cloak and cut it in two. He gave half to the beggar. Soon afterward, the beggar came back to Martin in a dream and said that he was really Jesus Christ in disguise. Jesus told the angels of Martin's good deed.

▲ In this old painting, St. Martin uses his sword to cut his cloak in two.

Martin decided to become a priest. Soon, he was made a bishop. However, he was so shy that he hid in a farmyard when he heard the news. No one could find him until some geese started cackling and gave away his hiding place. Because of this story, St. Martin's day is connected with one particular kind of food: roast goose. This is still the traditional meal to eat on November 11 in Germany.

Food at Martinmas

In the Middle Ages, November was a busy time. Farmers never had enough food to keep their animals through the winter, so many animals were killed on St. Martin's Day. The meat was dried and salted to keep it from going bad.

Today, on St. Martin's Day, people remember the stories about the saint's good deeds.

▲ Baked apples are a popular autumn food around St. Martin's Day. There is a recipe for this dish on the opposite page.

Baked Apples

EQUIPMENT

Apple corer
Cookie sheet
Strainer

INGREDIENTS

Four apples   Cinnamon
Handful of raisins   Nutmeg
A little butter   Confectioner's
                            sugar

Using the apple corer, take the core out of each apple.

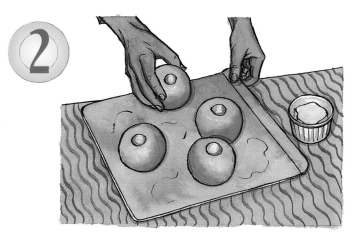

Put the cored apples onto a greased cookie sheet.

Stuff the hole in each apple with raisins. Sprinkle with a little nutmeg and cinnamon and put a dab of butter on top.

Ask an adult to bake the apples for 20 minutes, at 425° F (220 °C). When they are cooked, sprinkle with confectioner's sugar.

Be careful with the hot cookie sheet. Ask an adult to help you.

Advent and Christmas

▼ This huge electric Advent calendar is in Berlin. It counts down the days to Christmas.

Christmas, which celebrates the birth of Jesus, is the biggest festival of the year in Germany. The four Sundays before Christmas are called Advent. During this time, Germans enjoy getting ready for Christmas Day, on December 25. Many towns have special Christmas markets where decorations, presents, and Christmas foods are sold.

Christmas trees

The tradition of Christmas trees comes from Germany, and most German families have one in their home at Christmas. No one is quite sure how the tradition began. Some people think that the first trees were used as scenery for religious plays, which were put on at Christmas during the Middle Ages.

▲ Children at a Christmas market in Kayserberg.

St. Nicholas

In another European tradition that started in Germany, St. Nicholas gives presents to children. This tradition goes back several centuries. Today, on December 6, children still receive small presents from St. Nicholas.

▲ This picture shows St. Nicholas throwing apples to children on December 6.

27

Christmas Cakes

There are many delicious Christmas recipes. *Stollen* is a type of rich Christmas cake from the city of Dresden. It contains dried fruits and, in the middle, a thick layer of marzipan. *Lebkuchen* (pronounced "leb-cooken") are a cross between cakes and cookies and are made with spices.

▲ You can eat this little house. It is made out of *Lebkuchen*.

SPICE FAIR

Lebkuchen were invented in the Middle Ages, in the city of Nuremberg. Every year, the city held a fair, where merchants sold spices from far-off countries. These spices (ginger, cloves, and cinnamon) give *Lebkuchen* their special taste.

These cookies are called ▶ *Spritzgebäck* (pronounced "Shprits-gebeck"), which means "squirt cookies." The name comes from the way you squeeze the shapes out of a pastry bag when you make them. There is a recipe for these cookies on the opposite page.

Christmas Cookies

EQUIPMENT

Mixing bowl
Mixing spoon
Cookie sheet
Pastry bag and large star nozzle

INGREDIENTS

4 oz. (120 g) butter
$1/3$ cup sugar
2 eggs
$1^2/_3$ cups self-rising flour
Few drops of vanilla essence

Let the butter soften. Then mix the butter and sugar with a wooden spoon until the mixture is light. Add the eggs, flour, and vanilla.

Grease a cookie sheet. Put the cookie mixture into the pastry bag.

Squeeze small circles on to the tray in cookie shapes.

Ask an adult to bake the cookies for 15 minutes at 350° F (175 °C).

Be careful with the hot cookie sheet. Ask an adult to help you.

Glossary

Bakery A place where bread and cakes are made.

Catholics One of the two main groups in the Christian religion. The leader of the Catholic Church is the Pope, who lives in Rome, Italy.

Fertilizers Substances that make soil more fertile so it grows more grass or crops.

Floats Platforms on wheels, used in a parade.

Id-ul-Fitr A Muslim festival, held at the end of Ramadan, a month of fasting.

Kebab Pieces of meat on a skewer, cooked on a grill or barbecue.

Lent Period of 40 days just before Easter.

Pesticides Chemicals that kill pests, usually insects, that eat crops.

Pickled Preserved in salty water or vinegar.

Pita bread A type of flatbread that comes from Greece.

Protestants One of the two main groups in the Christian religion. The first German Protestants had a leader named Martin Luther, who left the Catholic Church in 1517.

Traditional Based on customs or beliefs that have lasted for many years. Traditions are part of the history of a country.

World War II A war between 1939 and 1945, when many countries in the world fought against Germany, Italy and Japan.

Picture acknowledgments
AKG photo 27 bottom; Bipinchandra 26, 28 top; Anthony Blake Photo Library *title page*, 13/Maximilian;
Cephas 5 mid right/Nigel Blythe, 6/David Burnett, 9, 10, 16/Nigel Blythe, 22;
Chapel Studios/Zul Mukhida 14, 18, 24, 28 bottom; Impact 7/Michael Mirecki; e.t. archive 23;
Robert Harding Picture Library 5 mid-left, 5 bottom right/Adam Woolfitt, 8; Pictor Uniphoto 22;
S.O.A. Photo Agency/Peter Thomann 27 top; The Stockmarket Photo Agency Inc *cover* and 5 bottom left, 12;
Tony Stone Images 20/Stephen Studd, 21/Joerg Hardtke; Trip Photo Library/B. Anthony, *contents page* and 17;
Wayland Picture Library 5 top left, 5 top right, 11.
Fruit and vegetable artwork by Tina Barber.
Step-by-step recipe artwork by Judy Stevens.

Books to Read

Amos, Janine. *Germany and German* (Getting to Know). Hauppauge, NY: Barrons, 1993.

Arnold, Helen. *Postcards from Germany* (Postcards From). Austin, TX: Raintree Steck-Vaughn, 1995.

Flint, David. *Germany* (Country Fact Files). Austin, TX: Raintree Steck-Vaughn, 1994.

Dolan, Sean. *Germany* (Major World Nations). Broomall, PA: Chelsea House, 1998.

Hirst, Mike. *We Come From Germany* (We Come From). Austin, TX: Raintree Steck-Vaughn, 1999.

Littlefield, Holly. *Colors of Germany* (Colors of the World). Minneapolis, MN: Carolrhoda Books, 1997.

Pluckrose, Henry. *Germany* (Picture a Country). Danbury, CT: Franklin Watts, 1998.

Pollard, Michael. *The Rhine* (Great Rivers). Tarrytown, NY: Marshall Cavendish, 1998.

Thoennes, Kristin and Cheryl Enderlein. *Christmas in Germany* (Christmas Around the World). Danbury, CT: Grolier Publications, 1999.

Index

Page numbers in **bold** mean there is a photograph on the page.